Kids Show Kids

How to Make Balloon Animals

Emily and Elizabeth Chauffe

casey shay press

For the counselors at
Kent Cummins Magic Camp
for teaching us how to make balloon animals

~ and ~

Limpy the Clown
for making animals for us since we were very small

© 2009 Emily Chauffe and Elizabeth Chauffe

ISBN-13: 978-0-9841879-0-4
ISBN-10: 0-9841879-0-1

Third Edition
Printed in the United States of America.

Hi. I'm Elizabeth. I'm seven.

My sister and I went to Kent Cummins Magic Camp last summer and learned how to make balloon animals.

When we tried to find books to help us learn more, we realized most of them were for grown-ups. So we made our own.

The balloon twists I included are pretty easy, although sometimes I had to ask my sister to hold one end while I twisted. And I still can't tie the ends of balloons after I've blown them up. That's hard! But everything else I did all by myself, and you can too!

I'm Emily. I'm ten.

I added some harder projects to the book. A few of them take several balloons to make.

We aren't afraid of balloons popping anymore, but we know you might be. So we added a POP warning by the steps that might cause the balloon to break.

Remember that you NEVER put a balloon in your mouth. If it pops, part of the balloon can get stuck in your throat, and even adults aren't safe when that happens.

Now turn the page and get started!

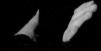

Getting Started

1. You will need to buy long skinny balloons just for twisting. Regular party balloons will not work. These balloons are very inexpensive, and you can get them at party or craft stores.

2. You will need a pump. These balloons are VERY hard to blow up with your mouth. Don't even try it!

Some pumps aren't made very well and will be frustrating to use. There are accordion style and ones with a handle. We personally like the handle pumps. Ours was only a few dollars. You don't need anything fancy until you go pro!

3. Stretch out your balloon a few times to make it easier to blow up.

4. Stretch the end of the balloon onto the pump. Make sure it goes far enough over the end. There is sometimes a ridge on the pump that you will need to pull the end of the balloon over.

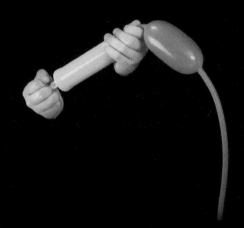

5. HOLD the balloon where it attaches to the pump so it won't fly off! Begin pumping air until the balloon has about four inches still empty. This gives the air a place to go as you twist. If you forget to leave space at tthe end, your balloon will POP! Some balloon projects need less empty space, so double check.

6. Roll the end of the balloon off the pump and let a little air out. This will soften it and make it easier to twist. You may have to ask a grown-up to tie the end of your balloon—tying is hard!

3

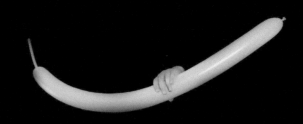

1. Blow up a balloon, soften, and tie, leaving two inches left with no air (see p. 3).

2. Pinch and twist a bubble about four inches from each end. Turn it at least five times. (Don't let go as you do the second one, or the first one will come undone!)

3. Twist the two ends together to lock them in place. Do at least five twists to make sure they will stay.

4. Grab the pinched ends with one hand and the big circle with the other, then push them together.

POP! Warning!

5. Twist the middle of the big loop into your earlier twist. Use at least five turns, so that the big circle becomes two wings. You'll hear lots of squeaking, but keep twisting.

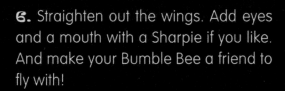

6. Straighten out the wings. Add eyes and a mouth with a Sharpie if you like. And make your Bumble Bee a friend to fly with!

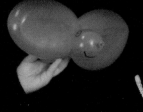

5

How to Make a Sword and Belt

1. Blow up a balloon, soften and tie, leaving three inches left with no air (see p. 3).

(see p. 3)

2. Bend the balloon in half. Make a loop at the end by twisting the two halves together. Make sure the loop is big enough to put your sword into later. You will have to pinch into the balloon as you twist, and it will make lots of squeaking noises. Twist it five times to lock the loop into place.

3. Wrap the long ends of the balloon around your waist, turning the loop to the back. Cross the free ends over each other to form an X by your belly button. Twist these ends together five times to lock them into place.

4. Turn the belt around so the loop is on one side, ready for your sword!

6

1. Blow up a balloon, soften and tie, leaving three inches left with no air (see p. 3).

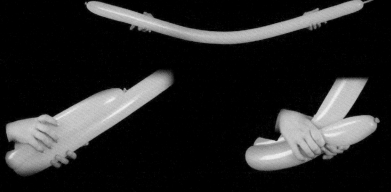

2. Pinch and twist the balloon about a foot from the tie end. Twist it five times.

3. Bend the balloon over so the twisted part is at the end.

4. Grab the two halves tightly and pinch them in, twisting them five times to lock them in place.

5. You should now have a big loop. Take the long end of the balloon and push it into the loop, pulling it most of the way through.

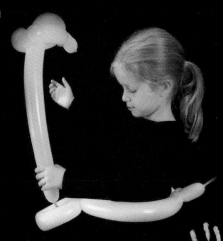

6. Hold your sword by the handle. Slip it through the loop you made in your belt and be ready for a quick draw!

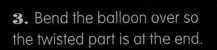

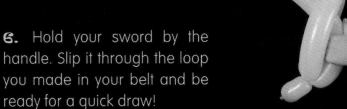

7

How to Make a Dog

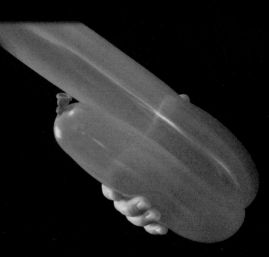

1. Blow up a balloon, soften, and tie, leaving four inches with no air (see p. 3).

2. Pinch and twist a bubble about four inches from the tie end. Turn it at least five times.

3. Bend the balloon at the pinch. This is about to become the dog's nose and ears.

4. Grab both parts of the balloon in your hand. Twist them together at least five times so they will lock. Don't worry too much about where to twist. Your dog can have a big nose and small ears, or a small nose and big ears!

POP! Warning!

5. Move the ears and nose around until it looks like a dog face. As you make all the dog's parts, the balloons may shift again, and you will have to move them back.

6. Decide how long his neck should be, usually about three hand widths from his ears, and twist five times.

Go to the next page!

7. Make a twist at the spot you chose for the neck. Remember to turn it five times! Then, just like the nose, bend the balloon in half, and twist both halves of the balloon together to lock them in. After making your five turns, your dog may be a little out of shape. Just get his nose pointing out, his ears pointing up, and his brand-new legs pointing down.

8. Now decide how long to make his body. Some dogs are L-O-N-G, like a dachshund. Others are short. You pick! Just like before, once you have made your choice, twist five times to start the back legs.

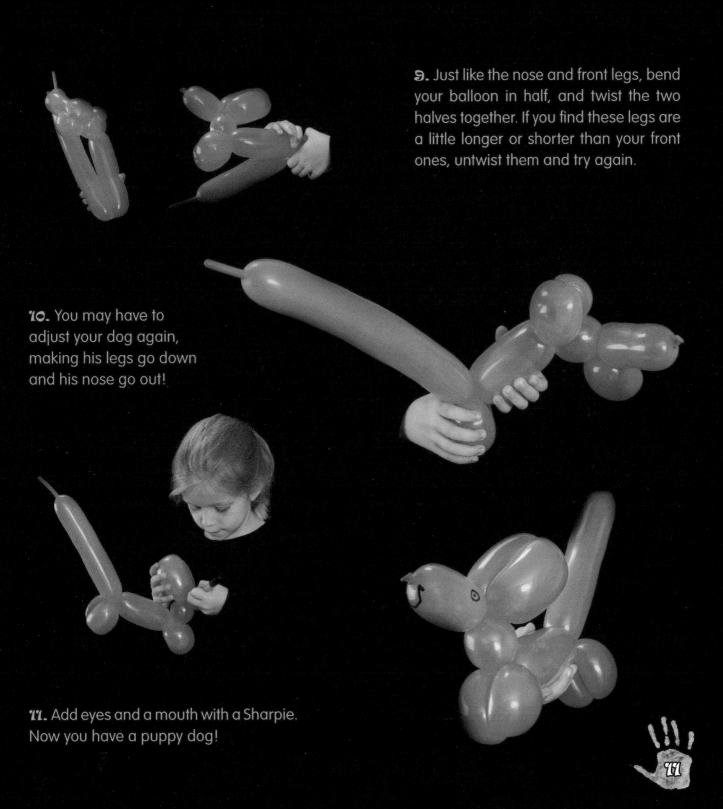

9. Just like the nose and front legs, bend your balloon in half, and twist the two halves together. If you find these legs are a little longer or shorter than your front ones, untwist them and try again.

10. You may have to adjust your dog again, making his legs go down and his nose go out!

11. Add eyes and a mouth with a Sharpie. Now you have a puppy dog!

How to Make a Giraffe

1. Follow steps one to five of making a dog on p. 8. The giraffe has the same face and ears as the dog.

2. Give the giraffe an extra long neck by making a pinch twist about fifteen inches from the face. Repeat the steps of the face to make the front legs, twisting five times for the pinch, bending the balloon at the pinch, then locking the two parts of the balloon together to make the legs.

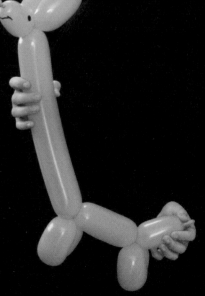

3. Twist again six inches from the front legs to start the back legs. Repeat the pinch twist, bend, and twist lock one more time.

4. Use a Sharpie to make eyes and a mouth on your giraffe's face.

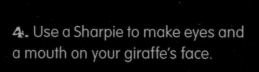

1. The elephant is really just a dog made backwards, so the extra for the tail becomes the trunk. Begin by following steps 1 to 5 of the dog on p. 8. The dog's face will actually be the elephant's back legs.

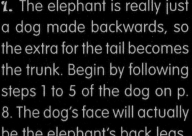

2. Make a new pinch about six inches from the back legs. Repeat the steps of the face to make the front legs, twisting five times for the pinch, bending the balloon at the pinch, then locking the two parts of the balloon together to make the legs.

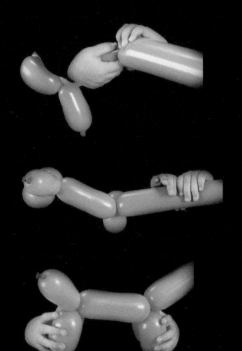

3. Twist again six inches from the front legs to start the elephant's face. Repeat the pinch twist, bend, and twist and lock one more time.

4. Use a Sharpie to make eyes and a mouth on your elephant's face!

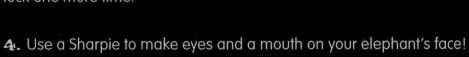

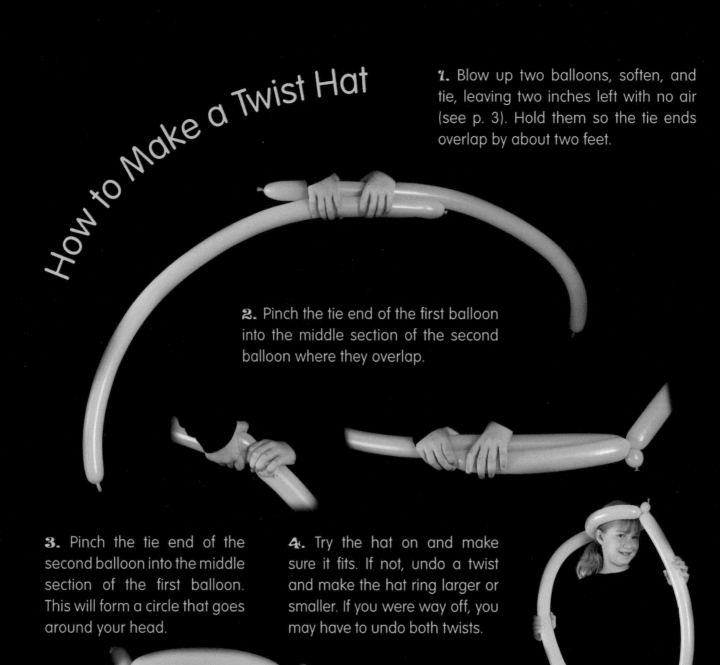

How to Make a Twist Hat

1. Blow up two balloons, soften, and tie, leaving two inches left with no air (see p. 3). Hold them so the tie ends overlap by about two feet.

2. Pinch the tie end of the first balloon into the middle section of the second balloon where they overlap.

3. Pinch the tie end of the second balloon into the middle section of the first balloon. This will form a circle that goes around your head.

4. Try the hat on and make sure it fits. If not, undo a twist and make the hat ring larger or smaller. If you were way off, you may have to undo both twists.

14

5. Take off the hat and begin twisting the two long ends of the balloons as if you were making a candy cane.

6. Continue twisting until you get to the end. You may have to hold the hat part between your knees or ask someone to help, as it will want to come untwisted at the bottom!

7. Pinch the two ends together and twist them five times to lock them into place. Your hat is ready to wear.

1. Blow up two balloons, soften, and tie, leaving two inches left with no air (see p. 3).

2. Pinch the two balloons together on the tie and twist five times to lock into place.

3. Cross the two balloons and begin a loose twist. Continue twisting until you get to the end. Pinch and twist the two balloons together at the end to lock them in place.

4. To get your candy cane to curve, squeeze it on the bend and rub it on your shirt to soften the balloons. You may have to do this several times before it stays when you let go.

How to Make a Wreath

1. Blow up three balloons, soften, and tie, leaving two inches left with no air (see p. 3).

2. Pinch the ends of all three balloons and twist them together five times to lock them in place.

3. Braid the three parts of the balloon. Cross the right balloon over the center balloon. Then cross the left balloon over the center balloon. Continue that pattern until you get close to the end.

4. Pinch the ends of all three balloons and twist them together five times to lock them in place.

POP! Warning!

5. This is the hardest part. Try not to get frustrated. You now have to twist both ends of your braid together to make a circle, all six balloons. Take your time, go slowly, until they are twisted well enough to hold in place.

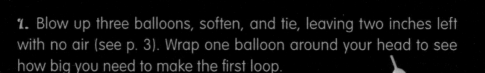

1. Blow up three balloons, soften, and tie, leaving two inches left with no air (see p. 3). Wrap one balloon around your head to see how big you need to make the first loop.

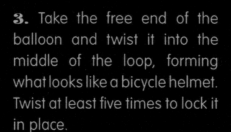

2. Pinch and twist the two parts of the balloon at the point you measured. Twist at least five times to lock them together.

3. Take the free end of the balloon and twist it into the middle of the loop, forming what looks like a bicycle helmet. Twist at least five times to lock it in place.

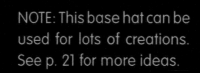

NOTE: This base hat can be used for lots of creations. See p. 21 for more ideas.

18

4. Bend the other two balloons in half and pinch at the midpoint.

5. Twist the balloons together at least five times to lock them in place.

6. Push the balloons through the top section of your bicycle helmet hat.

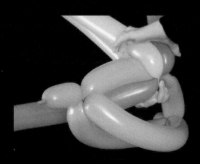

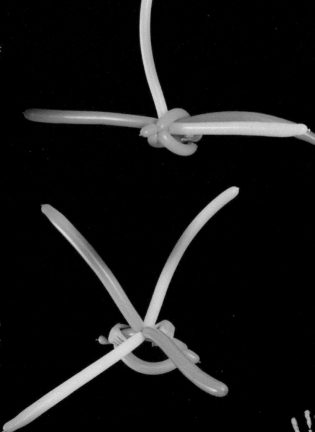

7. Twist the pinched part of the two loose balloons around the center of the balloon on the helmet so they are connected. Twist at least five times to lock in to place.

Go to the next page!

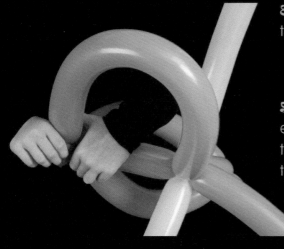

8. Take the end of one balloon and twist it into the front of the helmet, forming a loop. Twist it at least five times.

9. Repeat with the other end of the balloon, this time twisting it into the back of the helmet.

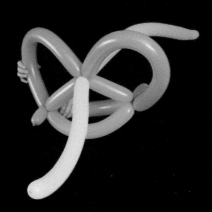

10. Repeat steps 8 and 9 with the second balloon, twisting the ends into the helmet to make two more loops.

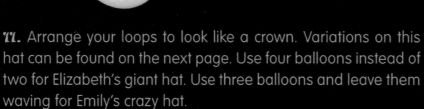

11. Arrange your loops to look like a crown. Variations on this hat can be found on the next page. Use four balloons instead of two for Elizabeth's giant hat. Use three balloons and leave them waving for Emily's crazy hat.

Make It Your Own!

All the ideas in this book are just the starting point. Once you know how to pinch, twist, and lock, you can do anything. It can be as easy as changing colors to make a wreath for the Fourth of July. Or like these hats, where we added balloons, or let them go wild instead of twisting them down. Or like the flower bouquet, where we just took balloons we'd messed up and shaped them into something new. The main thing is to have fun!

To find out more about Emily and Elizabeth
(they also do MAGIC), grab a grown-up and visit them at
http://emilyandelizabethshowkids.blogspot.com

21

CPSIA information can be obtained
at www.ICGtesting.com
Printed in the USA
451147LV00005B/6